THE STATIONMASTER'S DAUGHTER

THE STATIONMASTER'S DAUGHTER

Stella V. Le Neve

The Book Guild Ltd
Sussex, England

The Book Guild Ltd
25 High Street,
Lewes, Sussex

First published 1997

Set in Times
Typesetting by Keyboard Services, Luton, Beds.

Printed in Great Britain by
Bookcraft (Bath) Ltd, Avon

A catalogue record for this book is
available from the British Library

ISBN 1 85776 161 8

1

My life began on 2nd August 1924, the third child of six. Mary died at birth before me, so there was my elder sister, who was two years eleven months older than me.

At three I was sent to a convent school with my sister. We were baptised Catholics and went to the local Catholic church every Sunday. The school was a train journey away, and as my father was a goods clerk for the railway, we never had tickets. We were put in the train guard's care, travelling in his van at the back of the train. Some of the guards were nice, others teased us. I didn't like my nose being pulled, or being lifted down onto the platform on arrival and lifted up on the way home.

The walk up to the convent school was very rough and steep, with a sheer drop on one side down into nothing. There was a good wall though, so we felt safe. Sometimes my sister dragged me up the hill, occasionally she gave me a piggy back. She always bossed me about, but it must have been a worry for her, being 'in charge'. Later my brother joined us. He was full of life and tried to walk on the wall, with we girls shouting, 'Get down our Geoffrey'.

The nuns were excellent teachers; by four years old I had learned to read and was given a lovely doll on my birthday as a reward. I can still remember how that doll smelt, and what beautiful clothes she wore. I still love dolls and wish I had kept my treasures.

My mother came from County Durham, the ninth daughter of ten girls and two boys. We loved to go and see Grandma and all our aunties and uncles, where there were lots of cousins to play with. There was a great attic at the top of Grandma's house with a stage at one end and large boxes of old dresses, curtains, trousers and jackets to dress up in. We acted in plays we'd written and invited all the aunties and uncles to watch.

Grandma was a proper lady, who always wore a black dress and a lace cap over her hair. She kept a ribbon drawer and as a special treat she'd open it and find ribbons for our hair or pieces of lace to hand sew round our handkerchiefs. Every grandchild was made to feel so special and I never saw her get cross or shout. It was great to be told by Mother we were going 'home' to Grandma's. Nearly all our holidays were spent there and father enjoyed it too, as he could go out with our uncles for a 'drink'.

My younger brother was born when I was five, and when I was seven and a half years old, my mother had my last sister. It was in February, a cold, bitter winter. We were all told to go to the station (opposite the house) as Mother was too ill to bear the noise of our games. We sat in the waiting room all one day, looking through the window at our house and seeing the nurse rushing in and out, then the doctor. We did jigsaws and drew pictures, but the day dragged on and on. The porter had a big fire going in the waiting room but we were still cold. The train passengers came and went and still we stayed there, creeping back home at bedtime. On the third day we saw a smile from the window opposite and knew something had happened at last. The nurse came to tell us we had a baby sister. I had learned how to tell the time during that long wait, clock watching.

Mother was still very poorly a week later when we were asked, 'Where is your mother?' The priest had been to our house and demanded my mother get up and go to church to be churched – blessed after her childbirth. She was far too ill – the doctor confirmed this – and there was a dreadful row in Mother's bedroom with my father shouting 'Get out' to the priest. Father was a Church of England man; he had agreed to have us brought up as Catholics and had some tuition into 'the faith', but never went to church with us. The outcome was we were all taken away from the convent school. I remember Sister Mary Paul hugging me and saying, 'be a good girl always'.

It was a shock to be sent to the local church school. Prayers were said but how different they were. The head-teacher was the most awful woman, strict with a hard, unforgiving face, so different from the serenity of the nuns, and she seemed to dislike me on sight. My elder sister had gone to the high school and so I was the oldest in charge of my two brothers. I progressed well and was always chosen to play the lead in school plays. I loved acting and could remember all the words. My brother Geoffrey, however, couldn't do anything right. Dyslexia wasn't heard of in those days, and he was caned and made to stand in the corner because he couldn't do his writing and reading, even though he was clever at memorising and other things.

One day I heard shouting in my brother's class and looked through the glass partition to see my brother running round the classroom with the head chasing him. She hit him across the head and he ran out of the classroom and ran home. When I arrived home later Mother was in a temper. I told her I was sorry for

Geoffrey as the head was always nasty with him and hitting him. The outcome was a meeting with the school governors – the vicar, the headmistress, and one or two village people who 'governed'! My parents were called, and told that Geoffrey would be sent to a remand home if he misbehaved again! Mother was furious, but my father said, 'He'll be all right, he *is* hard to handle'. They came home and all hell broke out as soon as they were inside. My mother shouted at Father, 'Fancy admitting he's hard to control. You've no right to run your own son down!' The threat of the remand school really infuriated my mother – she knew the cause was our Catholic upbringing, which meant we just didn't fit in and talk like they did. The head and the vicar held another meeting the next day to decide what action they would take – my mother found out, went to the school and burst into this meeting and declared, 'You are discussing my children, I have a right to listen.'

She grew more and more incensed at the talk, stood up and declared 'I am taking my children away from this school.' The vicar said, 'Oh, but you'll be prosecuted. What other school will *have* them?' My mother said, 'None of your business', and left. She called on the way home to see Miss Bowden who had a private school almost across the road from our house. Mother talked terms and eventually this old lady agreed to take the three of us on. When Father came home Mother told him what had happened that day. He went mad, 'How the hell can we afford school fees?' Mother trembled and said, 'We have to'. There was an insurance policy due and that would pay our first term's money, but uniforms had to be obtained too. That weekend was busy – the boys had to have caps, me a Panama hat. She bought cap badges and a band for mine and sewed them on. The boys had new suits, I had a gymslip and there were ties for all of us.

Mother opened an account with the tailor and paid so much a month.

I think Father's parents helped; Grandma and Grandad were quite well off. Grandad was part owner in a colliery, but he had retired early with back problems. They came from the Potteries, living in North Staffordshire, and we saw them quite often. Grandma kept pigs and hens in their large garden and made everything. She taught my mother how to make jams, pickle, how to preserve everything, and how to make elderberry wine for our coughs. She was a strong and a large lady, rather over-powering, not the gentle 'Grandma from Durham' whom we all adored. Our little illegitimate cousin was brought up by Grandma, and she was treated pretty harshly. Yet Grandma was always kind to us and fed us well. The stigma of illegitimacy was awful – my father's sister had walked out leaving Grandma with her baby, and never contacted her. After I was given the doll by the nuns I showed it to Molly my cousin. She hugged it to her, and I felt so sorry for her I gave her my treasured doll.

We settled in at the private school. Lessons included French, when we would walk round her huge garden saying the names of flowers and trees in French. Playtime was in this huge garden too, though sometimes she would make us pick the fruit for her. She was very old to us, with loose teeth which she sucked while she spoke. She owned a very large cat which, every day without fail, would bring birds or mice to play with in front of my desk by the window. It would chew at them until they looked like a wet ball. I hated that cat and am now allergic to cats – if I get near one I cringe and if they touch me I come out in a rash.

2

When I was ten and a half my father was promoted to a stationmaster, and we were told we would be moving to a small station near St Helen's in Lancashire.

Being nearly eleven I was sent to the senior council school, my brothers to the junior. Father took me one day to St Helen's to yet another school where I sat an exam and was admitted to start the next week.

The Lancashire children spoke with their own accents and I was labelled 'stuck-up' and picked out for 'special' treatment. The new school was hard and strict, with a different teacher for each subject. I had a job to do *anything* right. The French mistress was particularly nasty; I was often dragged out to repeat French phrases after her in front of the whole class. After twelve months of this – my father had further promotion, thank goodness – and to Yorkshire we went. The countryside was lovely and we were sent to the village school alongside miners' children. They were very rough, in tatters some of them, yet Mother said their fathers earned more money than mine did, only they spent it in the pubs. 'Remember you are the stationmaster's children, you don't mix with them,' she told us, and we weren't allowed to ever make friends.

I joined the Girl Guides in the next village, Sandal. My father was abusing me so I went out as often as

I could, Girl Guides being the best excuse. I really enjoyed the meetings, the leader was so nice and taught us the flags of the world, Morse code, tracking and flag signalling – like the navy do. Then there were the songs too. On Sunday there was Church Parade and if you were chosen to carry the flag to the altar it was special and you felt so proud. When there wasn't a Guide meeting I'd tell lies, go out in my uniform and ride around the lovely countryside.

I was sent to the Commercial College three miles away at fourteen years old. My great aunts paid for my schooling; I was their favourite. Two wonderful old ladies – my father's mother's sisters, they had never married and were in business together, a cake and sweet shop. They made all the gorgeous cakes and sold the most delicious sweets and chocolates in their very high class confectionery business. They offered to pay for my further education and so I cycled three miles there and back for lunch, then home at 4 p.m., twelve miles in all and hilly all the way home. I was very unhappy, hungry and tired each day, then I noticed that my right side wouldn't keep still, no matter how I tried I couldn't hold my leg and arm still, the more the abuse went on.

One day I broke a lot of china taking a tray to my mother and father in bed. I got shouted and bawled at, then I told my mother I couldn't help it, 'My arm jumps.' She didn't believe it, but for once my elder sister spoke up and said, 'She's telling the truth Mam.' After a week or two the doctor called. I was getting worse by the day and scared to death, but still going to college as I dared not fail any tests. The doctor diagnosed St Vitus dance and said, 'She must be sent away from the home environment.' There were discussions and phone calls and – lovely! – I was sent to the aunties. It was the happiest time of my life. I was pampered and fed, a nurse came every day and I gradually began to get better. I took the neighbour's dog out on long walks, and had peace and deep sleep at nights, it was wonderful. The time came though when I had to go home. I was sad to leave, but welcomed back by my family.

Before leaving for the aunties I had sat my exams and had passed shorthand 80 WPM, and typing 60 WPM so I could get a good job. They were hard to get however. I tried lots of places but the war was imminent and few firms were recruiting, so I went by train into Leeds and was taken on in a warehouse selling wholesale goods.

The war started when I was fifteen years old, and the bombing started soon after. I travelled to Leeds on the train every day to work, then they cut down on staff and I wandered around Leeds looking for another job, not daring or wanting to go home until I had one. A small dress shop took me on as a book-keeper–assistant. The wage was very small and I was poorly dressed, still wearing my school blazer and hand-me-downs from my sister – she being of smaller build than me her dresses clung to my body. After some months my mother came into the shop. She must have felt ashamed – she actually bought me a green coat from the shop; what a different girl I felt!

At sixteen I tried my best to join the army – my elder sister had joined up and loved it, and I felt if I didn't get away from home I'd go mad. My father had left me alone since I returned from the aunties but I was so scared of it starting again. I was growing up and knew now that he had committed a terrible sin to me. Every time he looked at me and smiled I cringed and worried more. I filled in all the forms, gave my qualifications and waited. The letter came – I was not old enough, they regretted that I couldn't join until I was seventeen and a half years old.

I decided to try again and gave my birth as six months

older. The papers came for me to attend a medical in Leeds. When I went, it was very thorough. I noticed the MO gave me a long chest test, and in the forms it asked, 'Have you suffered any of the following?' – one was St Vitus dance. I put 'No' next to this, not realising then that it *was* serious. Anyhow more papers arrived for me, I was accepted and had to get the forms signed by my parents because I was only seventeen and a half – then the rows started. My father shouted, 'I'm not signing that!' and the rows went on for days and I thought for once I would have some say and when he went to his office the next morning I followed him. He looked up from his desk and I said, 'If you don't sign these papers I shall tell Mam what you have been doing to me all these years.' He went white and signed. Mother didn't know why he had signed them, he told her some lie obviously. I was free to leave. It was 1941, the war was bad and getting worse.

Food was getting scarce and everyone had their flower gardens made into vegetable patches. We also had pigs and hens, and a large piece of ground down the side of the rail track was used by my father. We helped, of course, and enjoyed it. The pigs were lovely and so clean – they are clean animals, always going to the same spot for their ablutions. They were like pets, but the time soon came for them to be killed for bacon and pork. The local butcher did the dirty deed and we collected the meat. Mother made brawn out of the head, nothing was wasted and we ate very well. We rubbed salt into the hams – we had a huge stone slab in the large pantry for this – then they were hung up on large hooks mostly in the bedrooms. The taste of home-cured bacon and ham was out of this world. The fat was always used – bread dipped into the pan after the bacon was cooked tasted marvellous. We collected waste food and stale bread from the shops to make the swill. All peelings, cabbage, scraps of any food were used in a large tin over a fire outside, boiled, then the pigs were fed and enjoyed it. Then Mother decided she could make cheese if we had a Nanny goat – that arrived the week I left home for the training unit. It proved to be the best time of my life, I was free – or so I thought.

I was seventeen years old when I arrived at my first posting in Pontefract. The square was occupied with shouting men and girls in squads marching this way and that. My heart sank; some girls were being bawled out for not doing this or that right, we all cringed, some looked lost, I froze. However, a kindly voice said, 'Come on girls' and we were put in groups, led into a very large building with rooms holding iron beds, each with three squares piled up at the top – 'Pick your bed, leave your case and come with me.' We were taken over – do this, do that, try this for size – we were hardly given chance to breath. Blankets, sheets, pillow case, then uniform: into line to be kitted out, and what clothes, I was so thrilled – after wearing my sister's cast offs all my life, and her being of a slimmer build, to get something that fitted *ME*. 2 tunics, 2 skirts, 1 cap, steel helmet, gasmask, and the underwear – even bras (I'd never had one – didn't have any bust to fill one anyway), vests, panties, khaki knickers – later to be called 'Passion Killers' – stockings. My feet were size seven and in shoe shops they used to say, 'nothing to fit your size' or they were far too expensive, so I wore plimsolls mostly or sandals. My new army shoes were just wonderful: lace ups, all leather brown. I never thought I'd have two pairs as well as plimsolls for PT and PT shorts and tops in a brownie-beige colour.

We all carried our kit into the long room and had to spread it out to check we had received everything and were told we were responsible for it and to look after it very well. I didn't need telling – I loved everything and at last I was proud of myself. When we all dressed in these new clothes there were titters: the hats looked odd and had to be pulled into shape, badges cleaned with brasso and put on, ATS badges on shoulders etc., then a sergeant came to inspect us all. Some like myself took to it all very well – others looked sloppy and had to adjust this and that. We were eventually taken for our first meal, which was super, though the creamed potatoes were sickly – later I found out they were mashed with tinned evaporated cream. I had always liked and still do like potatoes, but didn't like those. When I could I asked if I could have mine unmashed and got them. Sleeping that night was difficult. The three parts to the mattress were called biscuits, and we laid them side by side longways to make our beds. They creaked and groaned and, being a light sleeper, every time a girl turned over I woke up, and some girls talked nearly all night. They were all from different backgrounds, some common as my mother would have called them – the type we had never been allowed to mix with. I found it fascinating. Some of the girls could hardly use a knife and fork. We soon paired off and made friends, although for the initial training we were all together. It was tough and discipline was hard, but I loved every minute of it.

The lectures on various subjects each day were interesting – even the square-bashing I enjoyed after the first day. My father was ex-army and we were always made to be smart and walk with our shoulders back; when out walking he'd jab us in between our shoulders to make us walk right. This did help me, my enthusiasm was noticed and I was picked for 'marker' when my squad marched.

The training finished and I was posted to a searchlight headquarters on the east coast in Lincolnshire as a shorthand typist. There was a bomber base a walk away and we girls went to film shows whenever we could on the air field – the Lancaster bombers were magnificent, being loaded and serviced and setting off to distant places. It was 1941 and we were in the thick of the most dangerous time of the war. When I got back from the office one day we clerks were told to report to the firing range, handed great 303 rifles and taught how to fire on our bellies. We learned the hard way – the kick from the first bullet nearly put my shoulder out. At home my father had taught us to fire air-rifles so I knew how to aim and my eyesight was perfect. After so many rounds I was told I was 'good enough' and didn't have to report again, which was just as well, since we were uncomfortable lying there in skirts. The lads certainly had an eyeful.

For a few months I was happy there, though I couldn't see what good my clerking was, and there was hardly anything to do: nowhere to go when off duty, and we were miles from the nearest town. We were invited to the village to play whist; what an eye opener! The other players were old women, who took it very seriously. It wasn't a pleasure to play and after one evening I'd had enough. You had to play very seriously and not put a card wrong. I'd forgotten how to play, so they gave me awful looks and I blushed. The friend with me said, 'Never again,' and we went back to the bomber base, listening to the conversations of the Aussies, New Zealanders and our boys. We gathered that things were bad. The boys we met and laughed with went missing, and when we enquired about them we found out they had not come back off so-and-so raid. It was really getting to me – those lovely lads so full of life, chatting as they walked us back to camp – they were so happy to talk even now it haunts me. I remember their faces and pluck, their laughter, the way we struggled with them, the pleading, 'I'm off tomorrow' and then they'd gone.

3

One day after reading about our defence I decided I'd volunteer to go on Ack-Ack. They sent me for tests to see if, and what I was capable of. I passed and one day a posting came through to report to Oswestry in Wales. I'd hated office work, being forced to go to college by my father – now I faced more examinations, was issued with transfers, boots, battle dress, then sent for tests again. It was decided that I'd make a spotter (air-craft recognition), and in a group of twelve girls we were trained in a room filled with models of aircraft, and pictures, large and small, showing all different angles: front view, side view, every view imaginable. Gradually it all sank in, and even now, after 50 years I remember all the old planes. After lectures and training we dropped our hair, made up our faces and went to the NAAFI. It was full of soldiers and ATS alike, a piano played, people danced together, and the refreshments were awful rock buns and foul-tasting tea. Years later we found out they put bromide in it to stop any sexual behaviour.

After three months of learning and training, our battery was formed. By now I was 18 years old. I had noticed a soldier with very dark hair and brown skin watching me in the NAAFI every night. I hadn't taken much notice really – he seemed very shy and I wasn't interested.

We marched out with the band playing and passed a

complete battery of ATS and RA soldiers so proudly. There was every trade altogether, the officers lead and we followed. The troop train was waiting and we all embarked, none of us knowing where we were going. It turned out to be Yorkshire, a small, very hilly town. We were put into houses in the crescent overlooking the sea. The next day was a shock: all together we were marched down narrow streets, across the bridge to the 'steps', 199 of them. They said 'Fall out and climb those bloody steps' and we did twice a day, for what seemed like weeks and weeks. We fell on to the grave stones at the top exhausted, recovered and once more marched round the road, past the ruins of the old monastery and abbey then across fields where the guns were waiting overlooking the sea. What excitement, taking position ready to fire. After a while I spotted the plane, a Queen Bee we called it, towing a sleeve – the sleeve was the target. The first blast of the guns was a shock – I'd never been so near and they were 3.7 and big. The wind blew and blew, it was very healthy, the sea-air wonderful.

Time passed quickly in Whitby. The blustery sea air was wonderfully healthy, and the 'steps' became easier and easier. The grave stones at the top had names on and I noticed that one name was one of the victims in Bram Stoker's *Dracula*, which I was reading. Although the book is fiction, Stoker used the names of the dead, who were buried there.

We eventually took the train to our very first Ack Ack site, no one knew where. We filled the troop train and watched the scenery. After a while I recognised my area, opened the window and we sped through my village. I looked into my father's office, where he was sitting at his desk and I shouted 'Dad' but he never heard me. We arrived at Temple Mead's station, Bristol, then to our site on a hill. We stayed in long huts, two beds in each little section with a wardrobe between. We were on duty from that minute on, at a command post with four 3.7 guns. The alarm bells soon started and life became one mad rush. If you were in bed you pulled on clothes and tin hat, grabbed your gas mask and ran still fastening it and God help you if you were last.

Being a spotter I was more on the command post than the others, but when in action there were two of us, one reading angles and bearings, one following the target. My voice developed fast, shouting 'enemy aircraft', 'on target' to the predictors and height finders – there is none of that now, it's all automatic. It was much harder to hit targets in our day.

We really enjoyed our lives, except of course when we were overtired, our reward a mug of cocoa out of a bucket. We laughed and sang with relief when the raid was over and the danger had passed. The boys on the guns were much older than we girls. My dark-haired one was amongst them, still shy and I thought around 24. One evening we were dancing in the NAAFI to a gramophone record, he came across and asked me to dance. He was wearing plimsolls and hadn't shaved – I looked him over and refused, said I was tired, though I still danced with the other girls. I thought if he wants to dance with me at least he can look decent. We both laugh about it because soon after I saw him kissing an ATS corporal I couldn't stand. The next time he smiled at me I smiled back, he shot over the room to me and we danced a quickstep and he was very good. I loved dancing – we all did, though I let my hair down, which was long, and auburn, and curly. The corporal used to shout 'Get your hair off your collar', even though we were off duty but still we had to obey. It used to be fastened in a long bootlace, making a thick roll, and it was so nice to let it down. My hair always caused envy with the other girls.

My soldier eventually asked me out, and on our next day off we went into Bristol on the bus, then to the pictures. After that we always danced, went to the pictures, or sat together in the NAAFI with the others. Life was very pleasant. Eighteen months passed and life was hectic most of the time though the raids seemed to ease off. He asked me to marry him, by writing W.Y.M.M.I.L.Y. on a piece of paper, then he kissed me. We were alone in the rest room, we laughed and I said 'yes', not knowing or caring what the future held. I knew I didn't want to go home after finishing in the army, still being sick at heart at my treatment. Although I loved my parents I couldn't see me ever living with them again. On leave my mother was always miserable, Father had affairs, and she'd had blackmail letters. My boy had no prospects – he was a farm worker from a poor family with four sisters, two of whom were WAAFS. His mother lived alone, his father had died of war wounds when he was eleven. His mother had brought them all up by going out to clean. They had a different life from me, who was supposed to be so 'special' because Father was a station-master. Joining the army had given me freedom of action and I could look back and laugh.

At around this time my sister (in the army) had fallen ill; she was on a gun site near Brighton and was in hospital. On my next day off I went to see her, a long journey from Bristol. There was a raid on when I arrived with my 24-hour pass and my 10/- wages. I walked through the raid and finally arrived at the hospital – a long way in the pitch dark winter's evening. She was pleased to see me and looked poorly, they had to stop in bed during the raids, and luckily the bombs did not fall on the hospital. A few months later she was invalided out of the army and sent home.

I wrote home and asked if I could marry – apparently

all hell broke out. My father ranted and raved, said I was too young. Mother told me there were terrible rows. Before my sister left the army Father asked her to visit me and 'see' this soldier. She did and reported that he was nice – more upset. 'Nothing but a bloody farm labourer, a bloody farmer Johnny,' he swore. Of course I didn't know all this, life still went on at the camp and we were busy again, especially at nights. I wrote home and told my parents, 'You can please yourselves, there are ways and means to make you consent.' My sister wrote back saying they'd been beside themselves with rage but yes I could do as I pleased but not to expect any help from them! Six months later my father was promoted again and my parents moved to North Derbyshire.

My marriage was arranged in the village church, banns were called and I went on leave. Before this however, we were both sent to different army camps as our unit was split up. Action was needed on the east and south coasts more as the Doodle Bugs started. John went to Bexhill-on-Sea, and I went to Dovercourt in Essex.

This posting was difficult, moving from the wooden buildings in Bristol to the Nissen huts in Dovercourt. The cold in the Nissen huts was terrible. We stole coal to heat water to make an OXO drink, crawling under barbed wire to get it, and sat with our boots on the stove. The ice formed on the sea that winter and I yearned to get away. John came to see me and we were charged 2/6d for a room in the town and went and had a greasy, fatty butty in the café that was always full of army, navy and airforce personnel. The lady who let us have the room made us a cup of tea and apologised that she couldn't make us a meal as she only had her ration book – the sandwich dripped with fat and brown sauce – thick slices of freshly cut bread filled us.

The raids were dreadful which meant we were all

absolutely exhausted. Spotters were thin on the ground, and so I had longer spells on the command post than usual. It was a relief to get my marriage leave: 14 days with coupons to buy an outfit. Mother and I went into Manchester to buy what we could, but clothes were in short supply and everything was expensive. I eventually bought a grey costume but couldn't find any black or grey shoes so had to wear brown with my grey suit – awful. I didn't feel nice, but my sister gave me a hand-knitted short-sleeved jumper she'd made and a little hat trimmed with a piece of light grey fur, and father got me a corsage – an orchid, from a man he knew and I was ready. John had arrived the day before; Mother liked him, Father was very quiet. We lived in the Station House a few yards from the church, so Father walked me round, through a thick pea soup fog. John had his 50/- suit sent him from his sister, and looked so handsome. There were 40 guests and we were so happy, my lovely aunties came from the Potteries and Grandma. My mother's family didn't come from Durham, they were all tied up with the war. We spent our honeymoon at the Station House – when we counted up our money we had 25/- between us to last a week, so we walked the lovely hills of Derbyshire. One day we went into Manchester and had our photo taken in our clothes – the only civvies we had.

In no time at all it was time to go back to camp and our separate ways, upset at having to part so soon and longing for the war to end. I jokingly said after three months of everlasting action, 'I won't be here in three months,' the girls laughed and said how daft I was, but after a while I noticed I fancied pickles and anything spicy. John and I had managed to get 24-hour passes to be together in London and Portsmouth. He was being moved about all the time, but I stayed in Dovercourt. He managed to see me more often when he was sent to Felixstowe across the river; poor lad, he used to walk eight miles there and back and catch the train to Ipswich – we slept in the damp rest-room near a gun-post – no one knew we were there and the girls didn't tell, or I'd have been on a charge. When the alarm bells rang though I had to leave him. I still remember the damp smell of the put-you-up bed, and wonder how I managed to conceive our little girl. After five months I told the officer that I was pregnant and she was furious – we were short of spotters. I understood her, it was unbearable. When I was just three months pregnant – still running up and down the command post, I complained I felt ill, and was duly sent to the Medical Officer. I was so stupid I didn't know that a man made the baby, it wasn't talked about and I just hadn't thought.

The Medical Officer I went to see must have been in his sixties. I didn't like the look of him at all, and have hated him from that day since. A lance corporal accompanied me as it was quite a walk from the camp and I didn't know what to expect. 'Take your pants off and lie down', I was abruptly told. I was scared to death and embarrassed when he came round the curtain, raised my knees up and started to push his hand into me, up and up he seemed to go. I felt very faint and groaned, he took his time poking about. Then it was over and I climbed down, feeling drained and so ill that I nearly passed out. On the long walk back I felt wet – yes I was bleeding. That night I lay very still and the next day told the Medical Orderly I couldn't go on duty. As the beds had to be made every morning there was no lying down, so I sat huddled in front of the stove all day feeling very sick. It passed off however and again I had to do my job watching the sky, running like mad, dressing whilst on the run and it was quite a run from our Nissen hut. There was a prisoner of war camp in the field next to us, and as I walked with a friend past the Germans who were building a road with rubble to our camp, one of them squirted urine all over me. He did it so quickly without the soldier escort seeing him, but my shouting out made him take in what had happened. My uniform was soaked, I cried in temper and the Tommy knocked the German with his rifle butt. The Germans were always screaming, they were in tents and had no shelter to go in during the raids, and of course shrapnel was always flying about. But I had to go back to camp feeling very low.

My discharge papers were to be signed – I was pregnant. It's a wonder: I swear to this day that MO tried to abort my baby. When I was so ill carrying Stella Bernadette and having her in St Mary's hospital in Manchester, I was asked if I had been abused badly. My husband was told he was very lucky we both lived and I was not to have any more babies.

My father came up with an idea, he proposed that I become a crossing keeper on the railway – there was one empty a mile down the track from my parents' with a little house, two up and two down, wage 12/- per week, hours 7 days a week 12 hours a day, 6 a.m. to 6 p.m. I jumped at it; my own home and 12/- a week sounded wonderful, not realising the loneliness and frustration of not even being allowed to go for a walk. The ground was very, rough, but I eventually grew flowers and some veg. I had 30/- a week army allowance for our daughter and myself, which was enough to manage food on; the rationing was still bad, mostly we ate potatoes, I remember frying them, boiling them, roasting them in the fire. There was no electricity, only gas, and I bought a gas geizer so that we had hot water. I scraped up enough money to buy a three-piece suite, the double bed was given to me and I made rag rugs and stained the wooden floors. However, that first winter was very cold. The house shook, the rugs lifted with the wind and the drafts were awful. The engine drivers used to throw me lumps of coal as they went past so we had warmth and plenty of smoke, as the chimney blew the wind down.

I longed for John to be discharged. He was now in Germany, and our little girl was 6 months old when he was eventually demobbed with a lump sum of £82.00 for 9 years service gratuity money. He hadn't seen our home and when we walked as a family down the line to our little house we glowed with happiness, John carrying our baby while I somehow dragged the pram and his kit-bag along. He'd brought a lovely doll and underwear for me from France, but I had put on so much weight they wouldn't fit me, the stockings were sheer silk and did fit, thank goodness. I felt like a queen in them and darned and sewed them until I couldn't wear them any more. It was wonderful just the three of us. The next morning in bed he held our little girl above his head – she christened him with such a long wee he was drenched.

Straight away John decided he had to get a job and as he'd no trade, being a 'farmers' boy', he went down the track to the local cotton mill. The poor lad was given the job of bleaching all the cotton. He began to lose his healthy colour and started to have dreadful headaches, but he had to stick it, you weren't allowed to leave your job in those days. He earned £4.50 a week and being careful I started to leave my wages in the Railway Bank. His cigarettes – 10 Woodbines a day – were his only luxury, sometimes I wondered how I could afford them. But manage we did: I made our baby's clothes and John's lump sum bought all his clothes and kitted us all up for the winter.

The next winter was the worst ever – 1947. Every day we had to dig ourselves out to make a path up to the road 500 yards away, where the snowdrifts were 14 to 16 feet high, burying the gas lamps on the road – the village was cut off for weeks on end and we were a good 2 miles away. The sledge John made came in very useful, even baby had to be tied to it with the shopping – she loved it and laughed all the time. She loves the snow and wind even to this day, and living in Kent she longs for the snow and sledging fun we had. There were plenty of hills all around us, even up to the road it was steep.

John worked 6 years in that cotton mill and survived. He applied for another job and was taken on; it was more money but a bus ride over the hills to another small town. It was a Godsend and we managed well. When we eventually had a day off we would walk up the track, get on the train and go into Manchester, to the pantos and Ivor Novello's shows which were wonderful and such a thrill. At home we only had a battery wireless, that always needed charging with a WET battery, they called them.

When our little girl was three years old I had a weird experience in the night. John was on his 10 p.m. till 6 a.m. shift, and I woke up with the gas light from the top road in the bedroom seeming particularly bright. What woke me up was an old lady sitting on our bed, I'd felt the bed go down with her weight, she looked at me and I at her for a while then she smiled and stroked my face. She wore a frilly cotton bonnet and a shawl around her shoulders, and she kept smiling. I just kept thinking, 'Who are you? Where have you come from?, I wasn't scared and as I sat up she rose up off the bed, turned around and went to the door. It was closed, then as she went through it I realised, 'Oh, my little girl.' I lit our gas light, but the mantle was broken and the flame shot out. I thought baby would be scared if she woke up. I opened the door to pitch blackness, felt my way to the little back bedroom and found her sound asleep, under her 'Princess cover' – an Indian one I'd bought for her. I left the door open and I went back to the bedroom where the gas mantle still burned – what was left of it. I sat on the bed all night until John's bus arrived. I didn't tell him what I'd seen, he'd think I was daft or dreaming, but I knew it was all real.

The next day, the gangers (railway maintenance men) came along knocking in the pegs. They always talked, and made a fuss of me and our little girl. This morning the head man said, 'What's up lass, you're not your usual self, what's the matter?' He was a fatherly man so as the other men moved on I told him about my visitor. He asked me twice to describe her, then he said very seriously, 'Dunna worry lass, that was only Mrs Broadbent, she drowned in the well, or fell in it. They laid water into the house because of it. Her husband found her, maybe she fell in, no one knows, she'll not hurt you, she was a kindly old soul.' The well was concreted up 3 feet round and there was an iron grid on it. We filled it up with large stones, just in case our little girl pulled the cover off as she was very strong. I never saw the old lady again but the cupboard door in the back bedroom was opened every afternoon around 2 p.m. I just got used to closing it every day, until the builders came to plaster the room, they couldn't do it quick enough, it scared them to death. They'd watch it open with eyes like saucers – they did the plastering in quick time.

4

Years went by and I became more bored as John worked and our daughter was at school. We'd been told my life could be forfeit if we risked more babies, but I was so jealous of my sisters, they both had boys – I longed for one. I was 32 years old, so I told John we were too old now – he was 37 – and that I couldn't conceive at my age. Much to my delight I became pregnant and I knew it was a boy. I knew he'd have auburn hair with blue eyes and fair skin and be healthy and big – our doctor made me go back to St Mary's in Manchester, they were to decide whether or not the baby could be born all right. At two months pregnant I was kept in there whilst they did tests. Since my army days my blood pressure was very high, and there were other complications I won't go into, but they let me carry on with my pregnancy on condition that I went every fortnight, then every week, the 15 miles by ambulance to Manchester to see the gynaecologist. As time went on I grew bigger and bigger. They kept me in and with their wonderful care my baby boy was born, golden-haired, 10 lbs in weight, looking like a three-month-old baby. The matron came into the ward that night saying loudly, 'Now, where's the mighty atom?' so he was nicknamed that. Our daughter doted on him. I named him Christopher John – I'd always loved that name. Years later he was known as TOFFER to his sister and father.

When he was four and she fifteen and leaving school, I began to want more of life: the zinc bath, no toilet, no electricity, were getting to me. The grocer I went to in the village told me she was closing her shop – the property didn't belong to her, she'd rented it. I walked home day-dreaming 'if only' and the next day I went into town to the agents. They told me the property was £920 and I could have a mortgage if my husband would sign it and state his earnings. I was given the key and I persuaded John to go and look – oh the thrill! It was such a huge shop, with a house next door that continued over the shop. Then what a treat – a back bedroom turned out to be the biggest bathroom, all white with a 'toilet' and a huge 'walk-in' airing cupboard. It was out of this world with its lovely large rooms.

'*This is it*,' I decided. John was worried, 'How can we manage it?' I was scared too, but excited – his wages were good and I could sell *something*. I christened the toilet, then looked out of the large bedroom windows, with the village street and hills before me; I could see for miles. It is such a pretty village, spoilt now with a huge motorway. I must say to this day I still don't know how I had the nerve to do it. I went to a solicitor who was recommended to me. The bus journey seemed so quick (my little boy was with me). The solicitor was a sweet old man, and he told me £200 down and £720 mortgage as the agent had said. We went home, pulled out Railway Bank statements and found with some 2/- pieces, 2/6d pieces and 10/- notes I'd saved that we could just about manage it. There were no cheques for us in those days, so I drew the cash from the station and presented all the £200 to the solicitor. He smiled while he counted it. All the silver and notes seemed such a lot, I could hardly believe I'd managed it.

Above: All ready for our new private school, with my eldest sister

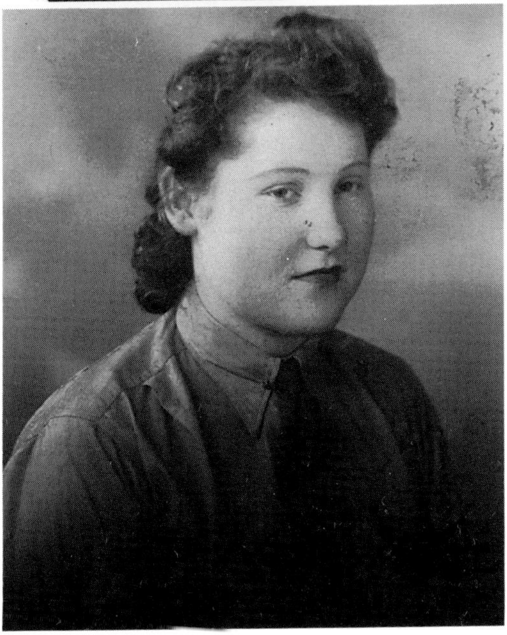

Left: Quite a new girl and loving it, 1941, aged 17 years

Above left: Rest camp, Weston Super Mare. Author on left

Above right: Intensive training, for action on gun sites, at Oswestry

Left: My Love, taken when he was 21, at Norwich

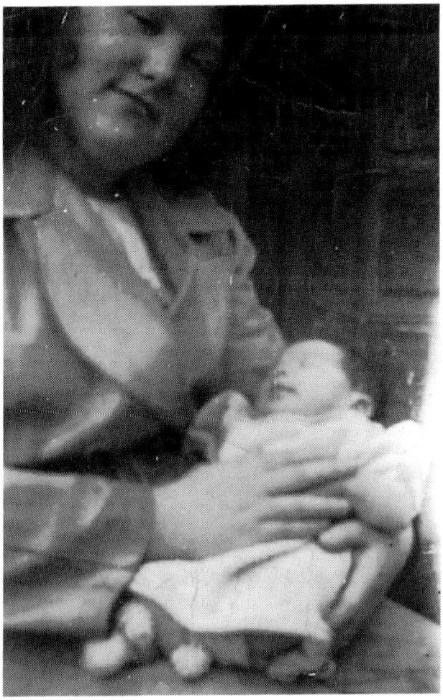

My first child, Stella Bernadette

Lantern Pike, behind the crossing house. My little girl waving Daddy off to work

Above: In the shop, 1968

Left: Our 50th anniversary – still together and happy

The property was soon ours and we started to clean it out, plastered walls, bought pieces of furniture and put them in and decorated. What excitement! The villagers wanted to know what we were going to sell – I told the truth – 'I haven't decided yet!'. We spent nearly a year doing it out and we left the crossing house after the windows were smashed by some schoolchildren. I never even told the railway bosses I'd left – they just stopped my wages. So after 15 years of two up and two down, no loo, no electricity and no sewage – it was heaven.

We concentrated on getting the house nicely furnished and carpeted. I love decorating and anaglypta was ideal for the old walls. We'd bought an old Anglia car and moved everything either on top or inside this. I was so pleased not to be tied to the crossing. I shouldn't have left my job between 6 a.m. and 6 p.m. but of course I had to sometimes with two children and schools. I felt free for the first time in my life after 4 years in the army and 15 years of 6 till 6 – no life except at weekends. Our little boy was five years old, and what a different life he was going to have compared to my lovely little girl.

My parents had moved to another station and so I was left in the village. My two other sisters were married, one brother lived in Leicester and my younger brother was a policeman three miles away from us. He visited us quite often and I loved him more than the others and was glad he was there with his family.

After doing all the house and shop up I wondered what to sell, then thought no village shop sold hot pies and fresh bread – only sliced stuff. When we went into the nearby small town to the market I always bought them for us as a special treat from the local baker – the smell from his shop was wonderful. So I picked one quiet day and went to see him. I knew him by sight, he'd always peeped at me between his piles of bread; I was quite an attractive woman – or so I was told many times. Anyway he came rushing around the counter when I asked to speak to him and I asked if he would deliver his baking the three miles to my shop. We didn't talk terms, he just grinned and agreed and I was rather embarrassed anyway. On the Monday we opened up. I'd told a few locals about hot pies, bread and cakes and was so thrilled when first one then another came and bought from me.

I had to refer to the baker's daily bill, where he put the retail price he charged me. He deducted a percentage off the whole bill and I paid him daily. After this had sold though I was quiet, so we started to serve tea and coffee – the shop was big enough for five small tables and chairs. Trade during the day was slow but at night the local teenagers came and sometimes caused trouble, putting salt in the sugar. Then early one morning a man tapped on the shop door. I opened it as he looked official with a briefcase, and he introduced himself as a wholesale grocer. After a while he persuaded me to let him supply me with an assortment of groceries. The very next day they arrived and at last all the shelves I'd painted and put up were filled. He said it would be a monthly account and not to worry: I could pay off what I could each month and he'd still supply me. The profits were 2d in a shilling – not much I realised. Even to feed ourselves I'd have to sell a lot. Every time we ate from the shop I wrote it down.

The sales of hot pies, tea cakes, etc. from my baker kept increasing, customers would wait for him. The shop was full of laughter, life was just wonderful – the black spot though was the café side. The village youths would sit with one drink all night, I'd be tired and they would be rude to our daughter, who was helping in the shop. Not liking this at all after about a year I sold the tables and chairs and we put up more shelves. I pondered what else I could sell, especially as the supermarkets had started in nearby Stockport and people were saying, 'Oh, beans are only so and so there.' I used to say, 'Well, by the time you've paid your bus fair it'll cost more, I can't buy as cheaply as they do.'

Then an idea came to me; there was no off licence within 5 miles of us. I didn't know the difference between beer, wine and spirits, but thought seriously about it, asked my brother for advice, and went to see a solicitor about getting a licence. It seemed to take an age filling in all the forms, but eventually I was to attend court to have a licence granted or not as the case may be. What a nerve-racking experience to have to swear in a witness box and be questioned. I shook with nerves and my knees knocked together – but with the result that I could have it, open 8.30 a.m. till 10.30 p.m. every day except Sundays and Christmas Day. I nearly dropped dead and was congratulated.

As I came out of the building a man came up to me – he said, 'I work for Tetleys brewery. Would you let us stock your shop for you? You'll earn a percentage of sale.' I just wanted to get home, so said, 'No, I haven't decided what I'm going to do.' Once you were in their hands you apparently worked for them, selling just their products – no one warned me but something told me to refuse. I'd walked away from him and was stopped by another well-dressed stranger and asked the same thing. When I arrived home my husband wanted to know everything – I don't think he approved somehow. Maybe I had been daft, I didn't know anything about drink, never having drunk it or been in a public house. I was 37 years old too and certainly couldn't afford to stock up with all that and still have to pay the solicitor's fees. We slept very badly that night; I was in a real tizzy not having been able to ask anyone anything.

In the morning I opened up. It was a lovely day and

there was a stranger waiting to come in. He introduced himself to me as a businessman from the next little town over the hill, he bottled Guinness and sold everything. We talked and he asked me questions – I was honest and said I knew nothing but was waiting for advice from my brother who was away on a sergeants' course. The questions and answers went on and on, and I rather liked him, he was a fatherly little man. The outcome was that he would fill all my shelves with every size of whisky, brandy, gin and everything else he thought I needed. I'd told him about money, but he obviously trusted me, and I accepted his offer to pay what I could every month end, and to buy from him his Guinness in particular.

The shelves were ready. The court had explained that one half of the shop was to be the off licence only, no food on those counters, only drink and cigarettes. The new stock arrived the next morning – box after box was carried in, crate after crate. The shop floor was full and I didn't know where to start. My daughter had joined the RAF, and had arrived home from Blackpool with an RAF boy she'd met, he'd offered to run her home which was lovely. She'd never been bothered with lads, this was her first. Anyway I was desperate and asked him if he knew how to separate all these bottles. He laughed and explained to me what was what and we stocked up the shelves – it looked very good too. We had a big cellar down some steps – the property had been a public house in the late 1800s – so the boxes and crates were piled up down there.

My very first sale was a bottle of sherry – I was a licensee at last! My name was over the shop already but now I had a licence I had to have it above the door *Stella Veronica Le Neve is licensed to sell* ... It was a thrill to see that sign over the door. A local man printed it for me. I'd asked him before the court and he'd done it already, sure I'd be granted the licence. Trade was slow at first but then people started to come for wine, and drink for parties. I had a good choice of all wines, but couldn't believe the snob value of certain drinks. When some villagers went on holiday to France and Spain they came in and asked for whatever they'd had there. It was so laughable – because they'd been abroad they were all connoisseurs, or so they thought. I sometimes wanted to laugh in front of them but being in this little village nearly everyone was related to everyone else. They called it, 'She or he ran up our alley', meaning they were so interbred they were rather narrow villagers – the older ones in particular. You were never accepted as one of them and to tell the truth I never wanted to be. Also there was a lot of jealousy – me a labourer's wife having a business – 'it wouldn't do well', 'no-one had ever done any good in *that* shop,' and 'who does she think she is?'

5

After my first five years I began to feel secure at last. I'd had to get a woman in to help me, as the cleaning was getting too much. She was a laugh though – the times I told her not to dust and smoke at the same time. Dropping ash everywhere, she polished the bedrooms and bathroom floor surrounds and left ash behind. It eventually sank in though and she worked well; she was a rough diamond (as we call hard workers in the north).

My husband was still working, but now his wages weren't subsidising the shop we were buying stock from the Cash and Carry and making much more profit. I still kept my accounts with my baker, wholesaler and bottler, I felt honour bound to, they'd been so good and helped me. After another five years or so, however, my wholesaler had stopped coming, the poor old man was quite ill, my bottler stopped delivering as he was short-staffed and so we bought almost everything from Stockport Cash and Carry. It was time to ask my husband to give up his hard job making brake linings. He did and took on the job of carrying the stock, so we bought a bigger car. I never left my shop, never wanted to, I was *so happy* meeting people: reps from all the cigarette firms, crisp companies, Rowntrees, the list was endless. Cigarette sales were huge so I had direct accounts with Wills, Players and Gallaghers. They were hard to deal with at first – in those days no women had had accounts without their husbands signing and agreeing to pay if they couldn't. I was furious: this was in the 1950s – women had the vote, I'd served in the armed forces and wasn't capable of running a village shop? The result was that I was allowed very quickly to have all the perks. Life was always a fight somehow, but I loved the challenge.

Then it was noticed that chocolate was disappearing from the large display counters. We had lots of children calling in off the school bus, and they were obviously covering up for each other and taking piles of chocolate. We were everlastingly filling up the stands, and the reps came every month to fill them up as well, and we were down on takings. There was a lot of pushing and shoving always and you just couldn't keep your eyes on all of them, so I had to stop them all coming in at once. Of course, after a short time the stock was lasting longer and any child that didn't want serving I told to stay outside. There were some nasty remarks but it settled down to a trickle calling.

With being a village in the Peak District National Park, weekends were very busy: hikers came on every train, stocked up with crisps and pop and set off up the mountains. Even in mid-winter the hikers came. We emptied large shop fridges of ice-cream and lollies every Sunday – that was our best day for trade as no where else was open, so I sold everything, meat, vegetables, cooked meats, bacon, to name but a few. Trade boomed and I began to feel my legs were giving out. I'd always had bad achy legs and just took tablets from the doctor. But now when I could sit down after 10.30 p.m. legs were so swollen and hurt so much I would lie on the settee with my legs up the back of it and cry. My doctor sent me to a specialist.

The orthopaedic specialist in Manchester, a very

famous man on the TV at that time, sent me for x-rays. I'd gone privately and it cost quite a lot. When he called me to tell me what the x-ray showed, he said, 'Good God girl, why have you let yourself get so bad? What have you been taking for the pain? Your knees have nearly gone and will never get better, you won't be walking in 12 months.' I told him about the little red tablets my doctor had prescribed for me, which I'd been taking for at least ten years. He nearly blew his top and read my doctor's letter and said, 'Stop taking these immediately. If you're not suffering from pernicious anaemia I'll be surprised, these tablets cause it. Come and see me every month at Buxton Cottage Hospital and we'll see what we can do. Give up your job and rest.' Ha, I thought – not on your Nelly.

I went to Buxton every month and on one visit he said, 'Oh yes, you're going to theatre.' I thought only operations were performed in them, but I was taken by a nurse to a ward and told to strip off and put on a gown. I shook from head to foot, 'What the hell were they going to do?' A nurse came back and I asked to see anyone who could tell me what was happening. I was told you have to go into the theatre because injections like these have to be done under clinical conditions, into the knee joints, and they would be painful and would maybe send me high. I thought, looking at the little operation outfit, open all the way down the back – that will never fit me, I'll be showing everything. I couldn't stand the embarrassment and anyway I had to drive home – a good run and in winter. I grabbed my coat and hadn't moved so fast since my war years. Of course, I'd discharged myself and after getting home was very frightened about treatment in future.

Another year or so passed and I was still on my feet, dosing myself with painkillers and losing myself in all the work. At night after closing the shop the pain was worse. Then the shop opposite mine was put on the market – my only opposition, the Co-op, had already closed. The shop opposite was a three-storey building, just a grocers', and I thought the trade was pretty good too. However, it didn't sell. Nearly a year went by and I thought, whoever buys it will take my trade, so after some thought I asked to see my bank manager (a friend of mine). He knew about the business and I said, 'I want to buy the shop opposite.' The property was £6,000 – today it couldn't be bought for £90,000 I'm told. Dave just said, 'Make your cheque out.' I told him I couldn't cover it all as all I'd done over the years was increase stock, but he said not to worry – make it out, so I did. I swore the agent to secrecy – not to tell anyone who the buyer was. People in the shop said '18's sold then, wonder what the new people will be like?'

We hadn't gone over to look until the day we signed the deeds. The little woman who worked there was always spiteful about me but when she saw me in that shop asking to see Mrs Reynolds, she nearly dropped. We were shown around my new property and what a grand place it was. All the carpets were included and every room except the kitchen was wonderfully decorated with anaglypta. Gosh I felt wonderful! Three floors and a wonderful large sitting room above the shop. We just hadn't thought about the house, but I decided then and there that we should move here. My legs and body were saying work less, and we moved over from the off-licence premises to the new shop, keeping both businesses going at first, then after a couple of months I let the old house to a young woman and child. This I regretted later as the place got quite filthy – she was just disgusting, of course, though I didn't see this for quite a while.

Running the two shops was hard work, my husband and I were hard pushed, although the woman who worked for me helped. The day we moved out of the off-licence all the weeks' takings went missing and the insurance didn't cover it. I'd left it in my overall pockets and it was taken from the pegs at the bottom of the stairs. I'd forgotten I'd left the money there – so careless of me. The worry was awful and suspecting people was worse, my trust in people had gone. On opening and serving the next morning one young woman my age who was in the local Dramatic Society with me said, 'My God, are you taking over the village? Will it be the Co-op next?' The jealousy was awful and did get me down, first one and then another – mostly people who only bought a loaf once or twice a week. My living wasn't made out of them by any means; keeping open until 10.30 p.m. and all day Saturday and Sunday was when we made our living.

Every time we changed the car – because of carrying stock this was often – there were snide remarks, about Rothschild etc. Little did they know the pain and worry I was suffering. My legs were worse and I'd noticed breathing was getting harder.

We decided to sell the off-licence and just have the grocers. It sold very quickly to a young couple, who saw the books, which were very healthy. The stocktaking professionals came and a valuation of stock plus property was agreed upon: £10,000. After 15 years or so the work had paid off, but we still had to pay £6,000 for the new shop. The interest was high on this and the grocery shop certainly didn't cover it. I realised what a silly madam I'd been, so after 18 months I decided to shut up shop, pay off the property and just live there, which we did.

We went to see my parents at Mablethorpe for weekends and I really enjoyed being free for the first time in my life – not tied to a crossing house or a shop was wonderful – not jumping up at every bell – like on the gun sites way back and in both shops. The realisation that there was more to life took over.

6

The Peak District in winter is very cold, my legs were very painful and although my chest occasionally was easy the bronchitis was causing me to cough. My young sister invited us to Lincolnshire, where they'd bought a cottage with a huge long garden – that was what I wanted. It was warmer there and not far from the coast. We went around and were told of a bungalow that had just come on the market for £7,250 with a quarter of an acre of garden, including apple trees – did we want to go and see? We did. The house was being emptied as the owner had died. It was brown with cigarette smoke but a lovely building – the roof made of Staffordshire tiles, and the garden was a wilderness – what a challenge. We hacked our way down the back garden, under the apple trees to the fence at the bottom. After the hills of Derbyshire this was good growing country and it even had a large greenhouse and shed too.

The woman who now owned it was giving stuff away and asked if we would like to buy the furniture. There was a mahogany bedroom suite and three-piece suite, dining chairs, tables, and a corner floor cabinet to name a few. She asked how much I'd pay and I said, 'Stop giving any more away – will £50.00 do? Just leave everything as it is.' She was relieved to be able to leave it to us, as the old gentleman was a relative. There was a woman throwing down bedding and lovely cotton sheets from the attic, which had a trap door and folding ladder. I told her to leave the rest – take what she had, I'd bought the rest, lock stock and barrel. I shall never forget her expression, sheer hate and greed. Apparently she sold stuff privately and the owner hadn't known, she thought it was going to charity. In the attic we found more furniture, a mahogany chest which this woman was emptying, apparently she'd taken all the Irish linen already and lace too.

As we had to get back to Derbyshire I left it with the agent to take care of, a nice elderly man who had taken to me. That was the quickest house buy we ever had: it was ours within 4 weeks. Our last shop and home went on the market for £10,000 including carpets and bedroom furniture I'd bought from the last owner. Another young couple bought it, actually customers of ours, and the premises now were just a lovely large house. We didn't make a fortune but had a shock because we hadn't separated shop and house fuel bills – we had to pay capital gains tax on both properties, which seemed so unfair after all that work – there was a Labour government and we were capitalists. The money was eventually paid, but my husband of course didn't have a job so signed on. But because, he'd been self-employed he received no dole money only his stamps were paid by the state. We realised he'd have to get a job somewhere, but there was nothing decent and he eventually went into a fertiliser factory working on a bagging plant for a pittance. We were back to square one, *but* owned a house and had a car and could manage – we felt like millionaires. I gardened and grew everything, we went out once a week into town some 8 miles away. The greenhouse was full of tomatoes, the garden became a potato plot, plus beans and lots more. The apple trees, although old, provided fruit for pies and there were also two pear trees, whose branches were so laden with pears every year they had to be propped up with forks. I lost track of time in my garden, we built a conservatory for the French doors and loved every free minute when we were at home.

Our son who lived with us was 17 at the time and out of work. He'd given up his apprenticeship to come with us. He had a scooter and eventually got into the local gang that sometimes went wild. We were glad when he brought a girl round as we thought it would stop him getting into trouble; they appeared a wild bunch and from things he's told me since they were.

My parents loved our place. They'd retired to Mablethorpe and Mother wasn't very well, she'd always been an invalid or pretended to be ever since I could remember. After they'd been to us they both decided they wanted to live near their daughters – my eldest sister was a widow and had moved near us. So we found them a semi – well *I* did, the other two couldn't have cared less if they came or not. It was a new house that needed painting so I did all the walls for them, their bungalow at Mablethorpe sold and we helped them move.

From then on life changed: they were always at our house and my sisters came too and their grandchildren – there was always a house full. There was jealousy, tittle tattle, and silly family rows that I just couldn't bear. We were the only ones with a car, so it was always, 'Do me a favour – take me to so and so,' and my job was being a chauffeur. John resented it as none of them ever thought of the cost of petrol and up-keep and we only had a small wage. We started to fall out; our son wouldn't go to work, he had seven jobs in no time, and the worry and unhappiness grew. I rued the day I sold my shops, my heart started to play up and I had awful panic attacks. My parents expected me to see them every day and sulked, 'where have you been?' yet if my elder sister was there they couldn't bother with me at all. Mum and Dad were always falling out and I was sick of being piggy in the middle trying to settle their silly rows. One day I'd had enough, went home and stayed away from them for two whole months – it was heaven. They all knew they'd gone too far.

Dad had a heart attack when he was 67 and was told not to eat any fatty foods. Mother held the purse strings, and *she* wouldn't go shopping, *he* had always to do it, the money only stretched so far and he bought everything, belly pork, fat meats. She was by now diabetic and had to have special food, she said, yet she'd eat chocolate cakes whenever they were bought for her, and three daughters provided it all. I felt sorry for my dad – he had to cook everything too whilst she sat and moaned. He gave her the lean meat and he had the fat. Talk about 'Jack Sprat could eat no fat', my poor dad couldn't have any lean and actually said, 'It's nice'.

Our money didn't stretch far enough to help but then my father had a very good railway pension, old age pension and pension for war injuries in the 1914–18 war. Mother saved, her handbag was stuffed and never out of her sight, and she hid money too and yet still complained they couldn't afford things. I felt so frustrated, one day when I took Dad into the local butchers, he started to buy belly pork for himself and steak for her. I said loudly, not thinking, 'For goodness sake, Dad, get something decent for yourself, you've plenty of money.' Unfortunately the butcher heard me and Dad was furious – he didn't say anything to me but blew his top to Mother. I was so sick of her penny-pinching and bossing him about, poor man did everything. Then I noticed knocks on his head, skin missing and I suspected she lashed out at him. We went down one day and as we approached the door I saw her lifting her stick to hit him, she stopped and pretended nothing was wrong, but I couldn't believe it. He'd always had these knocks on his head and had made excuses – being tall, he knocked it on a bus, bending down etc. – and I'd believed it all these years. I saw my mother in a different light. He fetched and carried for her and had to do the cooking and shopping. He retired at 60 years old from being a railway executive. As I say, he had a good pension too.

When they lived in Leicester, before he retired, my mother used to go to auctions, she bought some lovely things and sold them to the Americans. My parents' house was full of everything you could imagine, and the Americans came to the house and bought everything she bought. There wasn't much profit but she enjoyed it. After Dad retired she decided they should move to Mablethorpe, as the house they had in Leicester was rented from the LNER. At first they lived in a caravan, leaving all the furniture in Leicester, but then they found a nice bungalow and moved into that. At this time I had my shop and only saw them every three months or so, when we'd drive over for the day laden down with groceries and Brandy etc. There was never a proper meal but we always went to the fish and chip shop. We bought the fish and chips for my parents as well, and over the years I took car loads of groceries to them. My younger sister lived near them as her husband worked at the station. She said that Mother lived for months on the stuff I'd taken, but she never gave them anything. I couldn't believe she was so mean. Then, as I said, they moved near to us. My sister moved first, then us, then my sister from Derbyshire after her husband died. These years were the unhappiest, the friction and jealousies. Our 18-year-old son was a terrible worry and when they ridiculed him I fell out first with one and then the other, defending him and making excuses. My husband's wage was small and our son wouldn't stick at any job.

My father died suddenly. He'd said to Mother that morning, 'What day is it? It's something to do with America' – it was 4th July, he was 79 and had had a bloody awful life for all his retirement. He had to wear his old navy clothes from the railway all the time because she wouldn't provide for any more, except for once, a month before he died, she decided to buy him some trousers, a sports jacket and a nice hat – he wore them only once, on an outing I took them on. After he died I saw my sister's fellow wearing Dad's new hat and cried. He'd longed to wear civvies but because Mother thought he looked nice in his navy railway suits that's all he'd had for 19 years. He was 79 and he looked so pitiful in death, my heart nearly stopped. Mother had taken sleeping tablets so couldn't wake up, she'd refused to have a phone put in but she managed to go to my niece three doors away. I forgave him for everything that night.

Mother hated him for leaving her. She'd always played up, 'her heart hurt', her legs and everything else too and he'd looked after her all this time. She never cooked him a meal or made his bed, he slept in tatty sheets and bits of blankets in a single bed – she had their double one with all the good blankets on. I'd found out about his bedding when they both went down with 'flu and I looked after them both. We provided good bedding for him and I let mother know how disgusting his bed was (I couldn't let the doctor visit him in that state I told her).

After a year she started to get worse. I was going down every day to give her her meals, then early one morning the doors were all locked and I heard knocking from upstairs. We had to break in and then into her bedroom, she barricaded herself in that too – she'd had a stroke I think, said she couldn't get up. We called the doctor and it was decided I take her to recover to my bungalow. It was all right until she wanted to 'wee' – she couldn't walk so I padded a bucket for her to sit on but she fell into me instead, and started to cry that she hurt everywhere. I laid her down on the carpet, wrapped her up in the bedspread and went to my neighbour for help. The doctor thought she was faking it, and told her to 'get up'. I had to tell him she *couldn't*. He realised then I suppose, as he sent for the ambulance, and the hospital confirmed it was a stroke. As the ambulance arrived so did my elder sister and her daughter, and we all followed in our car. They treated her just for rest I think, she was 78 years old, still a very good looking woman and her skin was like a baby's.

After a while she was assessed, as they say, and allowed to come home. We moved her bed into her large sitting room and my eldest sister, who lived on her own, said she'd stay with her – she did for almost a week – then decided she had to go home to her empty house – some 8 miles away. It was left to me to nurse my mother, although I had a son and husband to look after. Every morning I'd drive down, clean up, dress her, feed her, and go home to cook her a midday meal, then back again, staying until tea-time was over, getting home in time to cook for my two men – then going back to Mother's to put her to bed. After a few weeks it got too much so I asked a woman who did 'caring' to call every morning, dress her and give her her breakfast and I'd do the rest – both my sisters objected, 'You're spending Mammy's money,' I was told. I told them in that case they could do it, and they soon changed their minds.

Life went on for a few more months and she seemed to get her faculties together, but then her toes were trodden on in an ambulance – result gangrene. I had no idea she was that bad. She was having the doctor and pills galore but I never thought of gangrene. She got worse, not being able to stand, and eventually they took her back to hospital. She'd refused all the time to have the operation, so now it had spread into her leg. I must have been in cloud cuckoo land – I never knew until my elder sister said, 'Ma's leg has to come off – otherwise she'll die.' The shock of it all – they'd all known and not told me! The outcome was they took her leg off and she was rambling when she came round, looking so frail, poor old Mother. She died a short time afterwards, it had spread all over her – what a dreadful way to go, her pain must have been unbearable.

7

A month to the day after we buried my mother I had my first heart attack. We'd always had my husband's sister and her husband to stay every summer for their holiday. While we had the shop my husband had his holiday and took them about while I was quite content in my shop providing meals and laughter for them. My husband's sister was a little queer, she'd had a car accident and been knocked out and afterwards said she was 'told' (she didn't say who by) to go to this or that church in Norwich where it would be explained to her. She was really weird, but I always listened to her tales, thinking she'd get better, which she did after her husband died of cancer. The poor man had been so patient with all her demands, go here and there, this church – all over Norfolk he drove her. We went to his funeral and she was normal – it made me think she'd been pulling the wool over everyone's eyes. I lost patience with her after that and couldn't bear to be bothered anymore. I had enough upset to contend with.

Anyway we went to Ashby market because she wanted some shoes off a stall. The day before I'd gardened, cut a quarter acre of grass, baked and cleaned ready for them. The pain started in my chest in the afternoon so I made myself a hot drink and sat up on the bed for half an hour until my husband and son's tea had to be cooked. The pain eased and we watched TV. They arrived early next day and as I helped her find three pairs of leather flat shoes the pain started again, worse than ever, though it had niggled between my shoulders all morning. I asked my husband for the car keys and told them I'd see them back at the car. Walking to the car park the sweat was pouring out of me I felt so ill, but I couldn't think why it was in my back.

It took them an hour to come back to me. I was sitting there with the car door open, people were looking in – I was embarrassed and looked away. We set off back home with my brother-in-law patting me on the back – I thought it might be indigestion, though I'd eaten nothing. We were half-way home and I told John to stop the car. I started to be sick and heave, I was wetting myself, the pain was so terrible. To the rescue came a lorry driver who was parked in the lay-by. He rushed over and ran straight back to his lorry, and the next thing I knew there was an ambulance and I was driven to hospital in Scunthorpe. I was taken into the emergency, where this little Indian woman doctor said, 'What you done to yourself?' in a strong accent. The shock, pain and silly question made me mad, the next thing I knew a sweet blonde little lady doctor was checking me over and assuring me, 'You'll be all right, keep calm, you're safe now.'

I was put in the emergency cardiac ward. It had six beds and I noticed all on the right had men in. I gasped, 'I'm not a man,' and they said calmly, 'No, it's a mixed ward.' I was there for ten days, wired up to machines. Every time I wriggled my toe the machine reading jumped about. The pain eased and whatever they gave me did the trick. I must have passed gallons of water as I lost 3 stone in 10 days. When I was allowed home I hadn't the strength to wind the window up in the car, that was the first thing I noticed. I thought, 'This is it. 57 years old and I've had it'. My sister-in-law and her husband left my husband to it, but she really upset me before she went home – she cleaned out all my drawers and wardrobe, even sorting out my knickers. She honestly thought I'd never recover. She went through all the kitchen cupboards and drawers, pan cupboard, the whole house and after sorting my clothes said, 'she had a lot of clothes, John.' I was livid! I'd had most of them for years, and half of everything there wouldn't fit me anyhow. I have never forgiven her; she did all this while my husband cried heartbroken thinking I was a gonner. Queer that her husband died of the same thing – a heart attack after a cancer operation.

Getting back to that sweet young doctor, all that first night in the hospital she was coming to check on me, even right up to the next afternoon. I said, 'Are you still on duty?' She said, 'Yes, I'm ready for a break now, another two hours.' Poor girl, she certainly saved my life and was so sweet. I never saw her again and wonder even now how she is, and if she is still a doctor, she was about 24, I should think. Another thing I remember about my trip back in the ambulance was the plump little ambulance man with a fat tummy over his belt; as he was giving me oxygen I was grabbing his fat tum – I do hope I never hurt him. He was very kind and apologising for all the bumps in the road, even outside the hospital there were road works going on. My mind kept telling me, 'You'll be OK if you get there.'

After a while John decided at 63 that he would take early retirement and be with me. He hated leaving me, he knew I couldn't keep still and rest, it just wasn't me to rest. He enquired and he could take it. He had worked since being 14 and then had 8 years in the territorials and army. We drew a pension that was rather measly but we managed. Then, what with the huge garden and greenhouse to look after, he decided to sell. I didn't want to but I knew he didn't like gardening. We looked around and found a nice semi-detached with three big bedrooms in a village near to Scunthorpe. Our bungalow sold very quickly – it would, it was gorgeous. The garden was a dream with all the work that I had done: the pond, the arbour and roses, the grape vine, the lovely almond trees we had grown from nuts, one 8 foot high now – all that work for someone else to enjoy. I felt like crying but knew it would very soon start to be neglected and that I just couldn't bear.

The new house wanted a new bathroom suite and lots doing to it, a pleasure to me since I loved colour schemes and choosing curtains and decoration. We had been in the house a week when this plump little woman came and introduced herself to me – John had gone down into the village. She was there for nearly three hours, talking about her husband who was ex army. She was a little younger than me and had travelled with him always – stationed everywhere, and apparently she was missing all that life as he now worked at an army base. Talk about nosy – she asked everything about us and stuck like glue, and started coming over to our house first thing every day. John was getting sick of it – she fancied her chances and made up to him. Her looks were awful, very hard features and all bottom. I am no oil painting but at least I know it; poor woman she became a real bore.

After three months I said, 'I've had enough – lets move'. We started to look for yet another house, not near any neighbours hopefully. Our bungalow had been perfect as we are content with each other. This poor woman just couldn't be insulted. The mail arrived one day and I'd opened the bank statement and left it on the kitchen table. She'd walked in when I was upstairs, she sat next to it, and straight away I thought, 'Oh hell.' As I folded it up she said, 'Oh aren't you comfortable? Wish I had your sort of money – just a thousand would be lovely.' She really thought I'd give it to her – the statement was declaring a balance after selling and buying our property. They had a mortgage and no wonder they lived it up – yet their car was on HP – we'd never lived like that and even today our daughter says, 'Please will you spend your money, we don't want it.' It was too hard to come by to waste. I still darn socks and mend, dye shoes, and renovate furniture – I enjoy it. I have a pair of leather sandals nearly twenty years old that were beige in colour, now black and look as good as new and are still very comfortable.

It was just twelve months later when we eventually moved yet again, to a much older house with character. It had beams, a lovely huge front door with brass studs and large hinges. Every downstairs room had delft racks all round the few antique plates we possessed soon looked lost, so we decided to collect and go to auctions. Once a month we went to the antique ones, plus household sales on weekdays. Gosh, we enjoyed it, and bought some very nice things and had somewhere to put it all.

This house was on a main road though, with a wall and small garden in the front, a Working Men's' club some 300 yards or so away. I'd put garden pots and hanging baskets out, and one night all my plants were taken. It was so strange, how did they carry that lot? After living there and not being able to garden, once again we decided to move back to the country. Before this I helped in a charity shop. There was some very good stuff given, the best however, went straight away into a room at the back where the manageress entertained her smoking pals, treating us volunteers as shop assistants. Through conversations with the others I decided to pack it in – I hate dishonesty – it was so obvious what was going on, so with two others we left her to do it herself. Apparently the charity caught up with her in the end. We always say,

'Charity begins at home' not with her though, yet she was paid too.

Once again we came across a bungalow in another village in Lincolnshire. It was smaller than our last one, two bedrooms, hardly any garden but enough front and back with a garage. We had lived in the house some 18 months, put in a new bathroom and were generally doing it up the whole time. But the traffic and noise outside was too much and being a light sleeper I hardly slept. Again the house sold quickly – we have always been lucky with buyers and eventually we moved yet again. Not feeling very well at all one night I had a terrible bilious attack, with unbearable pain – a gall bladder flare up they said. It eased off and we moved to our bungalow.

After a month or two this pain started again and I was rushed into hospital really thinking I was dying, sweating and shaking. My gall bladder was removed, and once more in the same hospital I had to recover. That was awful, being delirious most of the time I thought I was in a tent in a desert. They let me home after two weeks. My throat was awful and I felt dreadful. I had thrush all through me, and not being given a mouth wash, the infection had spread. Also I am allergic to penicillin so it took some time to clear up.

Car boot sales started and we enjoyed going to them – then decided to make a bob or two. We went to jumble sales, other car boot sales, and auctions and began selling at a good spot near Lincoln. It was so enjoyable being busy, buying and pricing things, getting up at 5 a.m. and setting off, having loaded the car up the evening before. We did very well and had people waiting for us as we unloaded, including dealers. The best sold very quickly and after a while everyone was getting in on the act, so we decided to sell just good stuff. Then chasing my grandson one day I broke my leg – they put a juet plate down it, knocking it into my hip with 5 large screws. I recovered from that OK but we stopped the car booting till I was stronger. The field we sold in was all ruts and I was scared of falling again. We stayed home and became very bored, then a vacancy came up in a hall not far away and we went every Thursday selling, only better stuff – more jewellery, which I love, the older the better. Gosh, I sold some nice things I'd bought in auctions. After doing this though for two years the council decided to close this hall down and we were 'out of a job' again!

My hip started to ache and then the dreadful pain started. My leg seemed to shorten, and the doctor just gave me more and more pain killers. I bore this for nearly three years until one day I said, 'I'll see a specialist, please'. The appointment was three months away, and I was in agony using a commode. My poor John had to help me up and down, I was useless all day and dreaded nights. Then I realised this was so bad I would phone the specialist's secretary and see if I could get in earlier – I did, and after an x-ray he told me the plate had fractured the hip and gone up through the cap above. He'd said, 'I won't be operating on you, one of my staff will', but after seeing the x-rays he said, 'I will be doing it myself.' The relief to know one of the best orthopaedic surgeons was going to do it was immense, to say the least. At 71 I was scared stiff, but couldn't wait for all the pain to be dealt with.

Then cancer appeared as a lump in my breast. I'd had it x-rayed three years before and was told it was probably fatty tissue, but now it hung down like a pear and ached and seemed to sh-sh as if it was alive and restricted in my breast. I talked to the damned lump, telling it it wouldn't be there much longer. The operation went OK, half my breast was gone but the cancer was a nasty one – malignant and likely to spread. I was sent for five and a half weeks radiotherapy once a day for a very short minute or so – no effects at all until the week after I'd finished it all, then my shoulder, neck, arm and breast felt achy and useless. I still can't stretch my arm up high, and every day I'm in constant pain from my back. I've had a scan and they decided my spine is a mass of arthritis, especially the bottom part. I walk with two sticks and am afraid to complain, it doesn't get any better at all. My thoughts are, 'Well, at 71 and having gone through this lot already, what next?'

I had had both my eyes done, cataracts removed and implants, before my leg broke. The specialist said, 'Yes they need doing, but it could be a year waiting – *but* I can do one next week privately.' So, being unable to drive and read, we talked about it – both eyes cost us £2,500, yet we are pensioners and have served our country well, always paying taxes, never once drawing any Social (as they call it today). It's a sore point, so when my leg was so bad I refused to go private – one quote I had was £9,000 – so really I've had my money's worth out of the health service and am grateful for it.

I'll close my story and miseries by saying that after being together for 53 years we love each other more every day. My old lad is 76 but tells me I'm so beautiful every day. Our daughter is well, happy and leads a very busy fruitful life. Our son is handsome, has had his problems with his marriage and caused us much heartache, mostly because of his two children being unhappy. Our only grandson is eight years old now, and we have three granddaughters: 27, 24, and 15. Both marriages are OK: our daughter's has lasted now for 26 years, son's for 17 years. He and his wife are both Leo's and argue and clash at times. It is all right at present, though often I've thought it never would be, but the poor children suffer too much with marriage break ups. If only people weren't so selfish.

When we started out together divorce was seldom thought of and abortions on the state to me are disgusting. In this day where there are those pills and condoms sold everywhere there is no need for girls to become pregnant, and have to murder their babies, unless the mother's life is at risk. Of course there are dreadful rapes; the cure for this and for child abusers should be immediate castration. When I mentioned this to an MP at my door he said very pompously, 'I'm a doctor and so can't think of doing things like that – it's against my profession.' What about those poor children? I'm afraid for the future with drugs, AIDS, and so on – in our day there was VD and TB to be afraid of, whole families died of the latter when I was a child. Now they say there are 80 cases in Sheffield again. Is history repeating itself? We are such a full country now; in my history lessons I remember the population was 28 million – now it's . . . God alone knows. How long can we manage and pay for everything and everybody? I'm keeping my knees, fingers and legs crossed.

Mostly I thank God for my good husband – that farmer Johnny, 'who still loves every inch of me,' he says, and there *are* a lot of inches, believe me.